Salamander or Lizard

How Do You Know?

WHICH ANIMAL IS WHICH? **?**

Melissa Stewart

Enslow Elementary
an imprint of

E **Enslow Publishers, Inc.**
40 Industrial Road
Box 398
Berkeley Heights, NJ 07922
USA

http://www.enslow.com

Contents

Words to Know

amphibian (am FIH bee uhn)—An animal that has a backbone and spends part of its life in the water and part on land.

moist (MOYST)—A little bit wet.

reptile (REP tyl)—An animal that has dry, scaly skin, lungs, and a backbone. It hatches from an egg that its mother laid on land.

tadpole (TAD pohl)—A young salamander, frog, or toad.

wetland (WEHT land)—Land that is covered with water for at least part of the year.

Do You Know?

Which of
these animals
is a salamander?
Which one is
a lizard?
Do you know?

Amphibian or Reptile?

Spotted salamander

A salamander is an **amphibian**. It lives in the water when it is young. Adult salamanders spend most of their time on land.

Collared lizard

A lizard is a *reptile*. It spends its whole life on land.

Wet or Dry Home?

A salamander lives in cool, **moist** places. You might find one under a rock or near a stream.

Northern red salamander

A lizard lives in warm, dry places. You might see one lying on a rock in the sun.

Iguana

Smooth or Scaly Skin?

A salamander has soft, smooth skin. The skin needs to stay moist.

Northern slimy salamander

A lizard has dry, scaly skin. The skin holds water inside the lizard's body. That is why a lizard can live in dry places.

Blue iguana

Four or Five Toes?

Fire-bellied newt

Most salamanders have four toes on their front feet. They have five toes on their back feet.

A lizard has five toes on all of its feet— just like you.

Green iguana

13

Tough or Squishy Eggs?

A female salamander lays lots of eggs in the water. The eggs are soft and squishy.

Red-backed salamander

Green anole

A female lizard lays just a few eggs on land. The eggs have a tough shell.

Tadpole or Young?

Marbled salamander tadpoles

A salamander starts life as a **tadpole**. It lives in the water. It grows legs and a tail. Then it moves onto the land.

A young lizard lives on land. It looks and acts just like its parents.

Five-lined skink babies

Now You Know

This animal is an amphibian.

It lives in cool, moist places.

Its skin is soft and smooth.

It has four toes on its front feet.

It hatches from a soft, squishy egg.

It lives in the water when it is a tadpole.

It's a salamander!

18

This
animal is
a reptile.

It lives
in warm,
dry
places.

It hatches
from an egg
with a tough
shell.

Its skin
is hard
and scaly.

It spends
its whole life
on land.

It has five
toes on all
four feet.

It's a lizard!

What a Surprise!

Red-spotted newt

Most salamanders rest underground in the winter. But red-spotted newts stay active. They swim in icy ponds and wetlands.

Some lizards have a trick for staying safe. When an enemy grabs them by the tail, they drop their tail and run away.

Blue-tailed skink

Learn More

Books

Arnosky, Jim. *All About Lizards.* New York: Scholastic, 2004.

Kalman, Bobbie. *Frogs and Other Amphibians.* New York: Crabtree Pub. Co., 2005.

LaBella, Susan. *Salamanders and Other Animals with Amazing Tails.* New York: Children's Press, 2005.

Fiction

Mazer, Anne. *The Salamander Room.* New York: Knopf, 1991.

Web Sites

Amphibians: Salamander & Newt
http://www.sandiegozoo.org/animalbytes/
t-salamander.html

Reptiles: Lizard
http://www.sandiegozoo.org/animalbytes/
t-lizard.html

Reptile Videos
http://video.nationalgeographic.com
Click on "Reptiles," then "Lizards,"
or click on "Amphibians," then
"Salamanders."

Index

Enslow Elementary, an imprint of Enslow Publishers, Inc.

Enslow Elementary® is a registered trademark of Enslow Publishers, Inc.

Copyright © 2011 by Melissa Stewart

Library of Congress Cataloging-in-Publication Data

Stewart, Melissa.
   Salamander or lizard? : how do you know? / Melissa Stewart.
      p. cm. — (Which animal is which?)
   Includes bibliographical references and index.
   Summary: "Explains to young readers how to tell the difference between salamanders and lizards"—Provided by publisher.
   ISBN 978-0-7660-3679-6
   1. Salamanders—Identification—Juvenile literature. 2. Lizards—Identification—Juvenile literature. I. Title.
   QL668.C2S78 2011
   597.8'5—dc22

                    2010003279

Paperback ISBN 978-1-59845-238-9
Printed in the United States of America
102010 Lake Book Manufacturing, Inc., Melrose Park, IL

10 9 8 7 6 5 4 3 2 1

To Our Readers: We have done our best to make sure all Internet Addresses in this book were active and appropriate when we went to press. However, the author and the publisher have no control over and assume no liability for the material available on those Internet sites or on other Web sites they may link to. Any comments or suggestions can be sent by e-mail to comments@ enslow.com or to the address on the back cover.

♻ Enslow Publishers, Inc., is committed to printing our books on recycled paper. The paper in every book contains 10% to 30% post-consumer waste (PCW). The cover board on the outside of each book contains 100% PCW. Our goal is to do our part to help young people and the environment too!

Photo Credits: Gary Meszaros/Photo Researchers, Inc., p. 20; © Mark Kostich/iStockphoto.com, p. 17; National Geographic/Getty Images, pp. 14, 16; Photolibrary/Oxford Scientific, pp. 15, 21; Shutterstock.com, pp. 1, 2, 3, 4, 5, 6, 7, 8, 9, 10, 11, 12, 13, 18, 19.
Cover Photos: Shutterstock.com

Note to Parents and Teachers: The *Which Animal Is Which?* series supports the National Science Education Standards for K–4 science. The Words to Know section introduces subject-specific vocabulary words, including pronunciation and definitions. Early readers may need help with these new words.